THE TREE

AT ROCKEFELLER CENTER®

A Holiday Tradition

THE TREE

AT ROCKEFELLER CENTER®

A Holiday Tradition

WITH TEXT BY MARTHA O'CONNOR

 TISHMAN SPEYER /  MELCHER MEDIA

PUBLISHED BY
MELCHER MEDIA, INC.
124 WEST 13TH STREET
NEW YORK, NY 10011
WWW.MELCHER.COM

IN ASSOCIATION WITH TISHMAN SPEYER
© 2007 TISHMAN SPEYER

TEXT BY MARTHA O'CONNOR
DESIGN BY ABBY CLAWSON LOW, LLC

PUBLISHER: CHARLES MELCHER
ASSOCIATE PUBLISHER: BONNIE ELDON
EDITOR IN CHIEF: DUNCAN BOCK
PRODUCTION DIRECTOR: KURT ANDREWS
PROJECT EDITOR: LINDSEY STANBERRY

10 9 8 7 6 5 4 3 2 1
FIRST EDITION

ISBN: 978-1-59591-048-6

PRINTED IN THE UNITED STATES

Contents

Foreword

As the literal and figurative heart of New York City, Rockefeller Center is a natural gathering place for those who live and work here and for visitors from all over the world. It's a kind of town square—a civic place whose history has been organically connected to the history of New York City and the United States since the early twentieth century. The Center's landmark art deco architecture, public events, artwork, and rich heritage have by all accounts made it an international icon. And the most dazzling moment during any given year at Rockefeller Center happens when more than thirty thousand lights come alive on the world's most famous Christmas Tree.

From the beginning, the Tree was a gathering place and a reflection of what was happening in the world around it. Even before the first formal tree went up, workers lined up beneath a Christmas tree on the Rockefeller Plaza construction site to collect their paychecks during the height of the Great Depression. Soldiers returning from overseas stopped by the center of the city to catch a view of a good old-fashioned Christmas Tree. People from around the world came after 9/11 to see the Tree decorated in a patriotic red, white, and blue. And families for generations have gathered in the Channel Gardens to take their annual holiday photos. Today, more than half a million people pass by the Tree every day, making Rockefeller Center the epicenter of New York City's holiday celebrations. • The stories highlighted in these pages celebrate the events that have become traditions, the months of work that go into bringing the Tree to Rockefeller Center every year, and the colorful personalities who make it all happen. You will see that the way things were done and the holiday style of the day often changed dramatically from year to year. Yet what has always remained constant is the class and quality of the operation and the people behind it. • As a co-owner of Rockefeller Center, TISHMAN SPEYER is a steward of this great place and its legacy in American and world history. We work hard every day to maintain the level of excellence demonstrated since Rockefeller Center's inception, from the first formal Tree celebration in 1933 to the many Trees that have followed. We are now upon our seventy-fifth Christmas Tree. It is Tishman Speyer's goal to enhance and safeguard this holiday tradition loved by all and establish a lasting mark that will live on for the next seventy-five years and beyond.

TISHMAN SPEYER, *Rockefeller Center 2007*

ROCKEFELLER CENTER, INC.

50 ROCKEFELLER PLAZA
NEW YORK

December 17, 1941

Members of your organization are invited to gather in the
Plaza at 5:30 o'clock on the evening of December 19th and
again on the evening of December 22nd to share with your
neighbors the candlelight processional and concert of the
Rockefeller Center Choristers.

Dressed in their robes of red and blue, carrying out the
Christmas lighting theme of the Center this year, the two
hundred men and women from tenant companies in Rockefeller
Center will make a colorful picture with their lighted tapers
as they march down the Channel, down the steps, and around
each side of the Skating Pond to the platform beneath the
tree. Here on both evenings they will present a half-hour
program of old-fashioned Christmas carols. In the event
either concert has to be cancelled because of too inclement
weather, a concert will be held on December 23rd.

This invitation carries with it our sincere wishes to you
and your associates for a Merry Christmas and a New Year
full of happiness.

Cordially,

Merle Crowell, Director
PUBLIC RELATIONS

A VIEW OF THE TREE AND THE CHANNEL GARDENS, 1954.

FOR more than seven decades, the Christmas Tree at Rockefeller Center and the holiday decorations adorning and surrounding it have taken on many forms. • Trees of different sizes, from a relatively diminutive twenty feet to a soaring hundred—the largest tree to date—have stood in the Plaza at Rockefeller Center. Lights, big and small, have adorned the evergreens, as have decorations in hues ranging from vivid Technicolor to understated pastels. No matter the style of the day, the Tree has always stood as a holiday beacon for millions of people around the world.

In each of these incarnations, the Tree has inspired, comforted, and thrilled those who make the pilgrimage to the center of Manhattan to participate in one of the city's—and the world's—most enduring holiday customs. Adults whose parents once brought them to see the spectacle pass on the tradition, bringing their own awestruck little ones to see the Tree. A quick look at the Tree over the decades reveals how the towering evergreen has evolved from year to year while deepening its roots as a holiday tradition. Generations to come will be touched by this breathtaking sight that is the heart of Christmastime in New York.

O Christmas Tree

A snowfall covers the illuminated Christmas Tree
and the statue of Prometheus in the winter of 1985.

Left: In December 1931, demolition men working on the excavation of Rockefeller Center pooled enough money to buy a Christmas tree. They set the twenty-foot high balsam fir amid the rubble of the future British Empire Building. It was draped with garlands handmade by the men's families from the tinfoil ends of blasting caps. A photograph, taken on Christmas Eve, shows solemn dirt-covered workers lining up to receive their wages from the paymaster. The cash box stands on an upended crate next to the Tree.

THE CHRISTMAS TREE

1933

1934

1935

1936

1937

1938

1942

1943

1944

1948

1949

1950

1939

1940

1941

1945

1946

1947

1951

1952

1953

1936 *There were two Trees this year: twin Norway spruces.*

1954   1955   1956

1960   1961   1962

1966   1967   1968

The Norway spruce, a typical species of tree used in the Rockefeller Center Christmas display, grows approximately ONE FOOT *each year.*

1957   1958   1959

1963   1964   1965

1969   1970   1971

1972   1973   1974

1978   1979   1980

1984   1985   1986

1975

1976

1977

1981

1982

1983

1987

1988

1989

1990

1991

1992

1996

1997

1998

2002

2003

2004

1993

1994

1995

1999

2000

2001

2005

2006

1999 *The tallest tree on display at Rockefeller Center was a* ONE-HUNDRED-FOOT *Norway spruce from Killingworth, CT.*

ROBERT AND WILLIAM LOUGHRAM, HURLEY, NEW YORK, 1963.

IT'S no surprise that finding a perfect Christmas tree for Rockefeller Center each year is a bit like a treasure hunt. · Charged with finding and selecting the Tree is the chief gardener of Rockefeller Center. It is not an easy job, and the task takes all year. He receives numerous photos and requests from people all over the country who hope their tree will be the chosen one. In fact, one year a Rockefeller Center Tree was found this way. · But often, the chief gardener has to go looking for the Tree. Every year, like a botanic detective, he takes to the skies in a helicopter and flies over multiple states, hoping to spot a magnificent tree out of hundreds of thousands of candidates.

1970

1958

1954

2006

1997

The Norway spruce is native to Northern Europe. Trees of this species can reach heights of 120 FEET. 25

The best trees are visited on the ground to see if they possess the character needed to be the most famous—and most photographed—Christmas tree in the world. The next step is a knock on the door of often unsuspecting owners by Rockefeller Center representatives, who in so many words explain, "We'd like to share your tree with the world."

The Tree Family

Left: The Robert Bragg family donated 1971's sixty-five-foot balsam fir from their farm in East Montpelier, Vermont. It was the first Tree to be mulched and recycled. *Below:* Ten-year-old Donald Snyder, whose father was an employee of Rockefeller Center, planted a five-foot Norway spruce in place of the sixty-five-foot tree that was donated by Mr. and Mrs. Fagg of Darien, Connecticut in 1954.

Selecting the Rockefeller Christmas Tree

So what makes a tree special enough to be anointed the Christmas Tree at Rockefeller Center?
According to the chief gardener at Rockefeller Center, some of the key winning characteristics are:

Typically (but not always) a Norwegian spruce

A height of seventy-five- to one-hundred-feet tall

A width proportional to the tree's height

Branches of a small diameter with an upward growth angle to ease the corseting process

Density of branches

Symmetry

"Dripping" branches, which look particularly lovely when adorned with lights

Healthy foliage

Beauty

An "it factor": that indefinable character, personality, or "star" quality

The Ideal Tree was the 1956 Tree, a white spruce, from Dalton, New Hampshire.

Corseting the Tree

Members of the B & E Landscape Company climb into the branches
of 1953's seventy-five-foot Norway spruce in order to corset the branches
before transporting the Tree to Rockefeller Center.

Prior to helicopters aiding in the search, other methods were enlisted to find the Tree. In 1959, a statewide hunt conducted by the Massachusetts Department of Natural Resources ended when the Tree was discovered by Harold O. Cook, the nation's oldest forester, on a farm in Podunk, Massachusetts. The state gave Rockefeller Center the Tree as a gift, and in return the real-life town of Podunk earned a place on the map. • The Trees themselves often possess a charmed history. The 1986 Tree, from the home of Mary and Vinnie Froeling in Nanuet, New York, had been planted by Mr. Froeling's father at approximately the same time that work on Rockefeller Center began in 1931. Ethel and Adolph Szitzar of Richfield, Ohio, planted 1998's Tree together fifty years prior and used it as their own living Christmas tree. And the first time Barbara Rickard saw the seventy-four-foot Norway spruce outside her new home in Stony Point, New York, she told her husband the tree was destined to be in Rockefeller Center. In 1997, the chief gardener came knocking.

Cutting Down the Tree

Above: A power saw is used to begin the process of cutting
1952's eighty-five-foot, eleven-ton Norway spruce.

Preparing for Transport

Below: The 1956 Tree is sprayed with a water-soluble plastic to keep its boughs fresh and green on its 335-mile trip from Whitefield, New Hampshire.

Desired dimensions are a minimum of 65-FEET TALL *and* 35-FEET WIDE; *however, trees* 75- *to* 95-FEET TALL *are preferred.*

The Christmas Tree at Rockefeller Center receives white-glove treatment on its journey to the heart of Manhattan. Send-off ceremonies in sleepy towns in New Hampshire and Maine are not uncommon. The Tree is frequently dressed in giant red bows or banners extending holiday greetings along the way to those who witness its pilgrimage. After a quick cut, the Tree is lifted by a giant industrial crane and gently placed on a specialized trailer. From there, trucks, barges, and even a plane have all helped the Tree make it to the big city, a voyage that takes place under the cover of night and—as befits any New York City V.I.P.—with a police escort.

A Gift from the Green Mountains

Mary Kelly of Dave Garroway's *Today* show interviews Vermont Governor Joseph B. Johnson, right, and the Plante family of Island Pond, Vermont, the donors of the 1957 Tree.

Before the Tree is cut down, its limbs are corseted over a period of several days.

The process reduces the diameter of the Tree to twenty feet.

This enables the Tree to travel down narrow roads and beneath underpasses.

A giant crane bears the full weight of the Tree when the process is complete.

The actual cutting of the Tree takes less than two minutes.

The approximate age of each Tree is verified by counting the rings in the stump left behind.

The Tree travels on a custom-made, telescoping trailer, which can stretch to 100 FEET *and can accommodate a tree up to* 125 FEET TALL.

1991   *The heaviest Christmas Tree to be erected in Rockefeller Center weighed approximately* 12 TONS.

Trees from Near and Far

Previous pages: The 1956 Tree traveled by flatbed truck from New Hampshire. The Saranac Lake peewee hockey team poses in front of 1969's Tree, a gift from the state of New York. *Right:* In 1995, the Sisters of Christian Charity donated the tree that stood in front of their motherhouse at the Mallinkropt Convent in Mendham, New Jersey. Several members of the convent attended the Lighting Ceremony in New York. *Below, left and right:* In 1998, a tree from Richfield, Ohio, was flown to New York City on the world's largest transport plane, the Anatov 124. Donor Ethel Szitar was on hand to watch as the Tree was loaded onto the plane.

Each holiday season at Rockefeller Center is a celebration of the search for the Christmas Tree, the people who generously shared their trees with the rest of the world, and the precise and one-of-a-kind process of delivering the Tree to its new home
And to think: all of this is just the beginning of each season's holiday magic in Rockefeller Center.

A Fond Farewell

The Elliott family watches their tree prepare for its trip to New York City in 1956. The sixty-four-foot white spruce stood in the corner of a field near their family home.

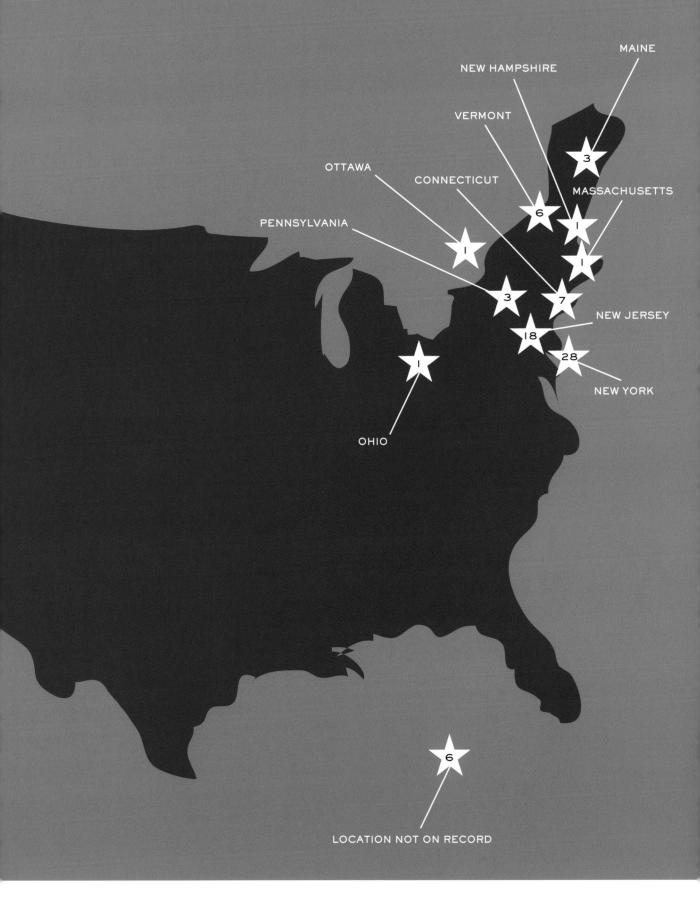

How Many Trees Came From...

MAINE

NEW HAMPSHIRE

VERMONT

OTTAWA

CONNECTICUT

MASSACHUSETTS

PENNSYLVANIA

3

6

1

1

1

3

7

NEW JERSEY

18

28

NEW YORK

1

OHIO

6

LOCATION NOT ON RECORD

1966   *The first Tree from outside the United States was given by Canada in honor of the Centennial of its Confederation.*

TREE HEIGHTS

From as nearby as Long Island and as far away as Canada, and spanning in height from twenty to eighty to one hundred feet, the Tree at Rockefeller Center is always changing.

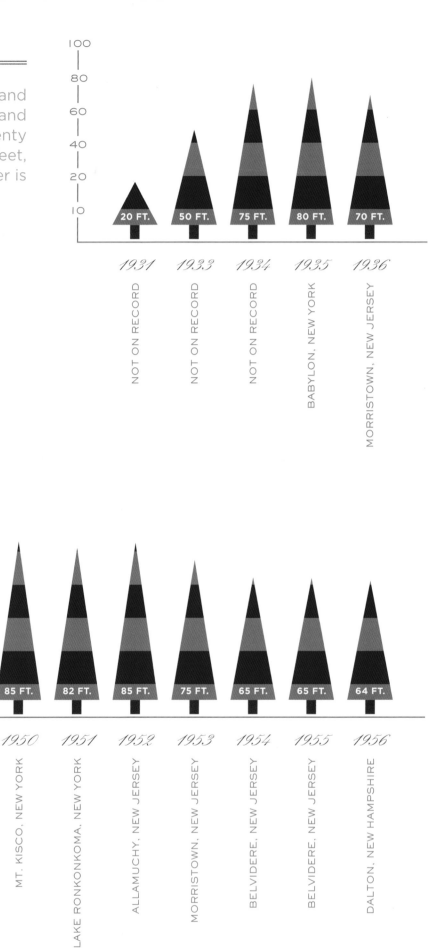

1931   NOT ON RECORD

1933   NOT ON RECORD

1934   NOT ON RECORD

1935   BABYLON, NEW YORK

1936   MORRISTOWN, NEW JERSEY

1947   DEER PARK, NEW YORK

1948   MT. KISCO, NEW YORK

1949   YAPHANK, NEW YORK

1950   MT. KISCO, NEW YORK

1951   LAKE RONKONKOMA, NEW YORK

1952   ALLAMUCHY, NEW JERSEY

1953   MORRISTOWN, NEW JERSEY

1954   BELVIDERE, NEW JERSEY

1955   BELVIDERE, NEW JERSEY

1956   DALTON, NEW HAMPSHIRE

1942   *This year saw three Trees in the Center:* one 50-feet tall *and two* 30-feet tall.

70 FT. | 70 FT. | 75 FT. | 88 FT. | 83 FT. | 50 FT. | 55 FT. | 65 FT. | 55 FT. | 85 FT.

1937 | 1938 | 1939 | 1940 | 1941 | 1942 | 1943 | 1944 | 1945 | 1946

ALLAMUCHY, NEW JERSEY | NOT ON RECORD | NEW JERSEY | HYDE PARK, NEW YORK | NOT ON RECORD | HUNTINGTON, NEW YORK | LONG ISLAND, NEW YORK | WEST ISLIP, NEW YORK | NOT ON RECORD | SYOSSET, NEW YORK

65 FT. | 64 FT. | 70 FT. | 65 FT. | 85 FT. | 67 FT. | 60 FT. | 60 FT. | 60 FT. | 64 FT.

1957 | 1958 | 1959 | 1960 | 1961 | 1962 | 1963 | 1964 | 1965 | 1966

ISLAND POND, VERMONT | EAST MADISON, MAINE | PODUNK, MASSACHUSETTS | NORTH HARFORD, PENNSYLVANIA | SMITHTOWN, NEW YORK | GREENVILLE JUNCTION, MAINE | HURLEY, NEW YORK | LAKE CARMEL, NEW YORK | DARIEN, CONNECTICUT | PETAWAWA FOREST, CANADA

47

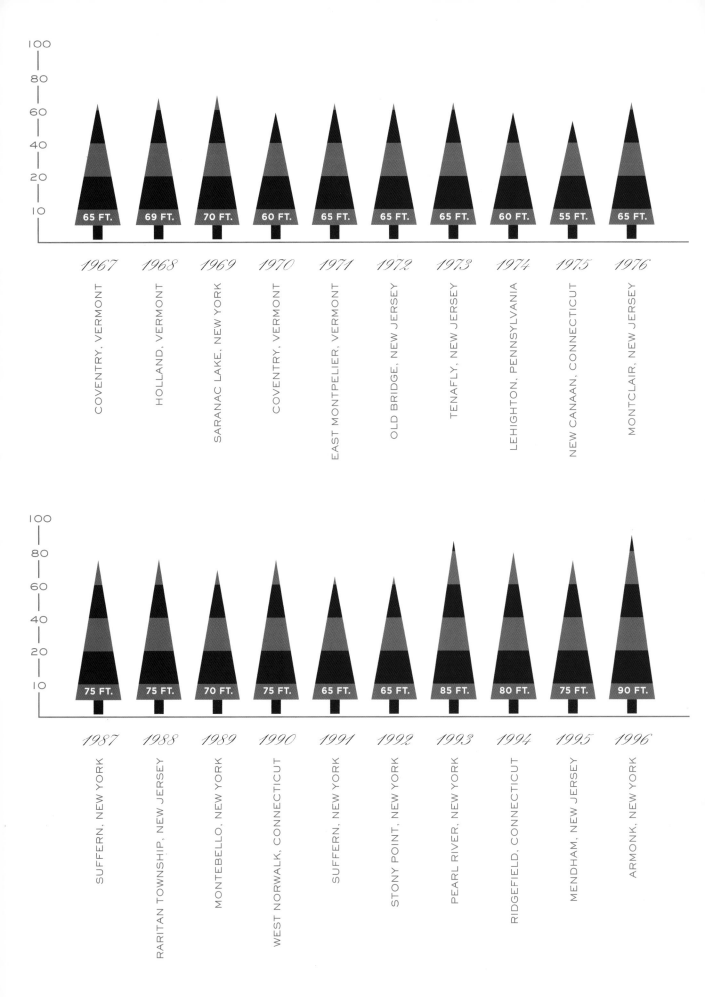

100
80
60
40
20
10

| 65 FT. | 69 FT. | 70 FT. | 60 FT. | 65 FT. | 65 FT. | 65 FT. | 60 FT. | 55 FT. | 65 FT. |

1967   *1968*   *1969*   *1970*   *1971*   *1972*   *1973*   *1974*   *1975*   *1976*

COVENTRY, VERMONT
HOLLAND, VERMONT
SARANAC LAKE, NEW YORK
COVENTRY, VERMONT
EAST MONTPELIER, VERMONT
OLD BRIDGE, NEW JERSEY
TENAFLY, NEW JERSEY
LEHIGHTON, PENNSYLVANIA
NEW CANAAN, CONNECTICUT
MONTCLAIR, NEW JERSEY

100
80
60
40
20
10

| 75 FT. | 75 FT. | 70 FT. | 75 FT. | 65 FT. | 65 FT. | 85 FT. | 80 FT. | 75 FT. | 90 FT. |

1987   *1988*   *1989*   *1990*   *1991*   *1992*   *1993*   *1994*   *1995*   *1996*

SUFFERN, NEW YORK
RARITAN TOWNSHIP, NEW JERSEY
MONTEBELLO, NEW YORK
WEST NORWALK, CONNECTICUT
SUFFERN, NEW YORK
STONY POINT, NEW YORK
PEARL RIVER, NEW YORK
RIDGEFIELD, CONNECTICUT
MENDHAM, NEW JERSEY
ARMONK, NEW YORK

60 FT.	75 FT.	75 FT.	65 FT.	60 FT.	70 FT.	75 FT.	75 FT.	78 FT.	68 FT.
1977	*1978*	*1979*	*1980*	*1981*	*1982*	*1983*	*1984*	*1985*	*1986*
DIXFIELD, MAINE	MAHWAH, NEW JERSEY	SPRING VALLEY, NEW YORK	SUFFERN, NEW YORK	DANVILLE, VERMONT	MAHWAH, NEW JERSEY	VALLEY COTTAGE, NEW YORK	FAR HILLS, NEW JERSEY	HARVEYVILLE, PENNSYLVANIA	NANUET, NEW YORK

74 FT.	73 FT.	100 FT.	80 FT.	81 FT.	76 FT.	79 FT.	71 FT.	74 FT.	88 FT.
1997	*1998*	*1999*	*2000*	*2001*	*2002*	*2003*	*2004*	*2005*	*2006*
STONY POINT, NEW YORK	RICHFIELD, OHIO	KILLINGWORTH, CONNECTICUT	BUCHANAN, NEW YORK	WAYNE, NEW JERSEY	BLOOMSBURY, NEW JERSEY	MANCHESTER, CONNECTICUT	SUFFERN, NEW YORK	WAYNE, NEW JERSEY	RIDGEFIELD, CONNECTICUT

SANTA AND FRIENDS WATCH AS THE 1951 TREE IS RAISED.

OF COURSE, it is the decorations that make the Christmas Tree at Rockefeller Center shine—both literally and figuratively. Icicles. Snowflakes. Pastel-hued globes and Technicolor ornaments. Even a coating of white sparkling paint to mimic frosty snow. All these and much more have adorned the Tree throughout its history. Regardless of what embellishments grace the Tree each year, its status as an iconic symbol of the holiday season is a constant. The visual splendor, the Tree's awe-inspiring size, and its sheer multitude of adornments—be they hundreds of wooden stars, thousands of twinkling lights, or yards and yards of aluminum garlands—have never failed to delight visitors from around the globe.

From Small Town to Big City

The 1963 Tree arrives at West 49th Street and Rockefeller Plaza.

The Arrival

Left: A seventy-five-foot Norway spruce arrives in New York City after a trip across the George Washington Bridge. The Morristown, New Jersey, Tree was cut and stored overnight prior to its predawn journey to the Center. *Above:* Trimmings for the Plaza arrive from Podunk, Massachusetts.

1997 *This Tree traveled down the Hudson River by barge from its home in Stony Point, New York.*

The process of decorating the Tree is a long one that involves dozens of electricians and many stories of scaffolding. As decorations become more elaborate, more time is required to dress the Tree. In 1941, the Tree was covered in eight hundred lights and took four days to trim. In 1950, workers began using scaffolding to aid in decorating. By 1960, the process called for twenty men and a period of nine days, and, in 1993, the time needed to trim the world's most famous Christmas Tree was more than two weeks. • From the improvised and humble beginnings of garlands made from tinfoil blasting caps created by construction workers in the Tree's first (unofficial) year of 1931, came ever-evolving, at times innovative, motifs reflective of their times.

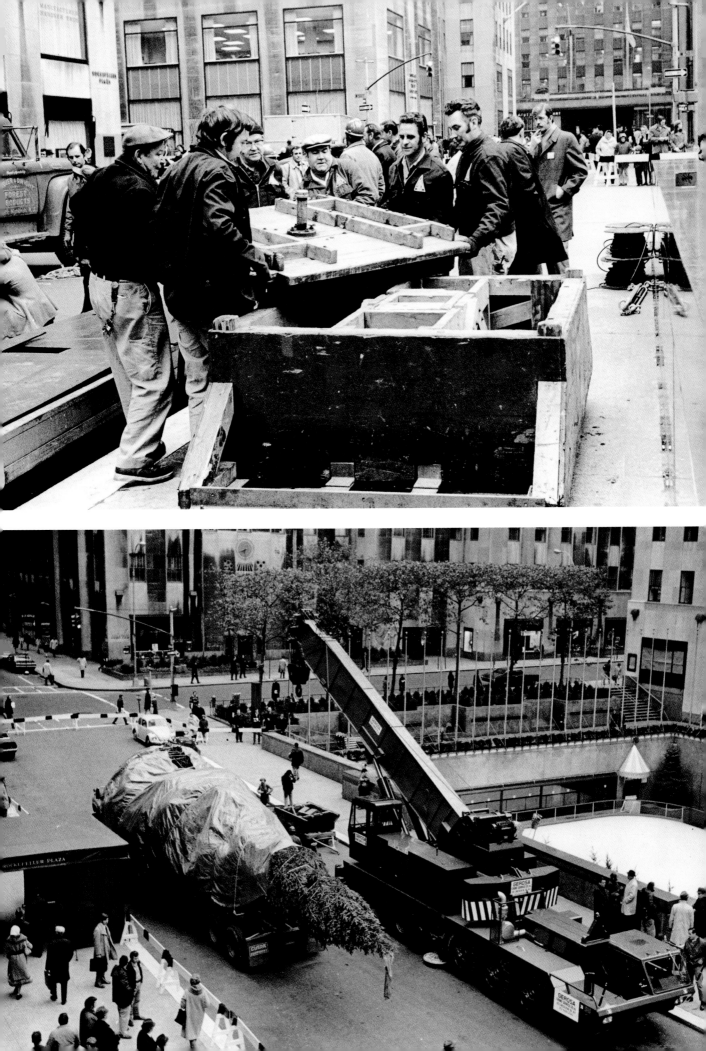

World War II ushered in an era of simple and patriotic designs, including red, white, and blue unlit globes and matching painted wooden stars fashioned in the Center's workshop. In 1942, no materials essential to the war effort were used to decorate the Center, and in the place of one towering tree, three more modest living trees were raised. From 1942 until the end of the war, the Tree went unlit each year due to blackout regulations. A defiant Mayor LaGuardia went on record voicing his disagreement with the edict, saying, "I know of no other period when lighted Christmas trees would be more appropriate."

Going Vertical

The sixty-five-foot balsam fir from East Montpelier, Vermont, is raised in the Plaza following a 320-mile trip. The 1971 Tree was found during the summer months on the farmland of Robert Bragg.

Raising the Tree

1

Once it arrives at Rockefeller Center, the Tree is lifted from its one-of-a-kind, telescoping tractor-trailer. Prior to its raising, a three-foot metal spike used to help stabilize the Tree is driven into the trunk.

2

The same 280-ton, all-terrain crane enlisted to remove the Tree from its original site is used to maneuver the Tree into position in front of 30 Rockefeller Plaza.

3

The custom-made crane is used to move the Christmas Tree at Rockefeller Center. The Tree is placed onto a platform with a thirty-gallon water basin.

4

The process of raising the Tree takes a full day and a crew of as many as twenty people. Four guide wires attached to surrounding buildings secure the Tree into position, with Center employees adjusting the tension on each to get the Tree "just so."

By 1945, postwar design featured an explosion of exuberant color, which Rockefeller Center's director of displays, Robert Carson, hoped would cause the Tree to "glow like a window of Chartres with sunlight coming through." Carson achieved the desired effect by painting seven hundred ornaments in fluorescent colors and bathing the Tree with new black-light technology, causing the globes to glow in the dark. As a result, the fifty-five-foot Norway spruce was dubbed "A Magic Tree." • In 1973, energy conservation efforts gave birth to decorations consisting of 2,850 multicolored ten-and-a-half-inch reflective discs, illuminated by a reduced number of miniature bulbs. • Following the attacks of September 11, 2001, the Tree once again served as a symbol of American pride and solidarity, adopting a patriotic theme that boasted thirty thousand red, white, and blue lights, while dozens of American flags took the place of the traditional silver banners hung around the Plaza in previous years.

Dressed from Head to Toe

Before a scaffolding system was employed to help decorate the Tree, workers affixed the star and ornaments to the uppermost branches before hoisting the Tree into place. Here, 1945's Tree is raised in front of the RCA Building.

Unloading the Tree

Above: Marc Torsilieri unloads the 1998 Tree at Rockefeller Center. For decades, the landscaping firm Torsilieri, Inc., and many other contractors and brokers have been involved in helping Rockefeller Center find, transport, decorate, and remove the Christmas Tree. *Left:* A member of the Torsilieri crew climbs in the branches of a corseted tree. *Far left:* After the Tree is set into place, it takes several days to decorate.

The present-day Tree is adorned with more than thirty thousand lights in five hues, and over five miles of wire is used in the decorating process. A nine-foot-wide crystal star by Swarovski, featuring twenty-five thousand crystals and one million facets, tops the Tree today, the largest star in the Tree's history. • While the majestic sight of the Tree trimmed in tens of thousands of multicolored lights is familiar to people around the world, the decorations have changed significantly since the first Tree was installed at Rockefeller Center. • The Tree's decorations continue to evolve with the changing times. Since 1996, Tishman Speyer has carried on the tradition by developing cutting-edge adornments for this piece of New York City history.

Crowning the Tree

With the help of the intricate scaffolding system, workers decorate the Tree in eight days. Here, the telescoping crane aids in gingerly placing the crystal Swarovski Star on the Tree.

BAY CRANE
BAY CRANE
BAY CRANE
TOP OF THE ROCK
OBSERVATION DECK
GLORIOUS 360° VIEWS
365 DAYS A YEAR
Rockefeller Center
THE
SWAROVSKI
STAR
ROCKEFELLER CENTER®
NOV. 14, 2006–JAN. 8, 2007
HOSTED BY
TISHMAN SPEYER

Scaffolding climbs the Trees from 1965 *(left)* and 1962 *(right)*.

ESTIMATE – CHRISTMAS PROGRAM – 1941

Purchases:

Christmas Tree	$ 500.00	
Colored bulbs for tree	135.00	
Bulbs for candles in windows	36.00	
2 16' wreaths for RCA Bldg. exterior.	140.00	
Greenery in fountains	75.00	
Muzak – carols, installation and		
removal	325.00	
Electricity refund to tenants	100.00	
12 small spot lights for pipes	20.00	
400 white-tipped pine cones	80.00	$ 1,411.00

Operating Department:

Refinish organ pipes	75.00	
Install and remove frames in fountains.)		
" " " Christmas tree......)		
" " " 2 wreaths on RCA Bldg)		
" " " 12 sets of organ)800.00 (?)		
pipes ....)		
" " " candles in windows ..	725.00	
"" " " Ornaments on tree ...	1200.00	
" " " Blue gelatins	75.00	
" " " 12 spot lights for		
pipes	100.00	2,975.00

Promotion:

Letters to tenants – multigraphing,etc.)		
Pictures)		
Posters) 200.00		
other expenses)		
Contingency	500.00	700.00

Estimated total ...... $ 5,086,00

Budget: $5,750

Today, each branch is individually wrapped in lights to achieve a dazzling effect, and there are no other ornaments on the Tree except for the Star on top.

The Star

Above: No Christmas tree is complete without something at its crown. Traditional finishing touches to holiday trees include angels and colorful glass finials, but it is a star, in one form or another, that has always graced the top of the Christmas Tree at Rockefeller Center.

Shining through the Years

Below: The star with the longest tenure made its debut in 1949. It was a five-foot-wide creation fashioned from Bakelite, a then-innovative material, and it gave off a translucent white glow. For forty-nine years, a custom-made crate housed the Bakelite star to ensure its safe return each Christmas.

The Swarovski Star

In 2004, an even grander Star crowned the Tree at Rockefeller Center. Swarovski's 550-pound Tree topper features twenty-five thousand crystals and one million facets, and its diameter is nine-and-a-half feet. The Star grew even more luminous the following year with the addition of L.E.D. lights to its center, making the Star look as if it were radiating light from its core to its tips.

Decorating the Tree

Right: Workers attach multicolored globes to 1949's seventy-six-foot Norway spruce. Dubbed "The White Tree," it was sprayed with hundreds of gallons of silvery-white, flameproof paint with the hope of achieving a snow-covered effect. *Below:* In 1944, four-year-old Patty Foster had the honor of placing the final snowflake ornament on the Tree.
Following pages: The final product in 1957 and 2005.

WITH its promenades and picturesque skating rink, Rockefeller Center is the perfect backdrop for a towering Christmas Tree. And the decorations surrounding the Plaza's celebrated centerpiece have long both complemented the magnificent evergreen and shined all on their own. • The holiday trimmings around the Plaza frame the majestic Tree with dramatic effect, whether a viewer emerges from the underground corridors of the Concourse or approaches the Tree via the Channel Gardens.

Previous page: Wreaths celebrating the holiday season flank the Atlas statue. *Right:* Radio City Music Hall glitters on a rainy winter night. *Far right:* Valerie Clarebout in 1954 with Robert Carson.

More than fifty years after they were created by British artist Valerie Clarebout, the white and wiry angels are as much a part of the Rockefeller Center Christmas experience as the Tree itself. Documented through countless personal snapshots and worldwide media coverage, the appearance of Clarebout's cherubs are synonymous with the arrival of the holiday season and the lighting of the famous Tree.

Above: *Valerie Clarebout's angels debuted at Rockefeller Center in 1954.* Opposite page, from top: *Clarebout in 1961 and 1958.*

2005

1949

1935

1956

Previous pages: A look at the changing decorations of the Channel Gardens, from simple garlands to glossy candy canes. *Right:* 1950's "Ceiling of Stars" sparkles over the Channel Gardens.

In addition to Clarebout's iconic angels, displays ranging from the understated to the whimsical to the sublime have occupied the Center's Channel Gardens and Promenade. In 1965, artist Karl Pehme designed stately, eight-and-a-half-foot gold fiberglass troubadours, which stood atop four-foot pedestals. At times the decorations were as elaborate as four live reindeer: Dasher, Prancer, Cupid, and Vixen spent the 1941 holiday season in custom-made rustic enclosures chomping on alfalfa hay and delighting visitors. • The Channel Gardens and Promenade have often provided the canvas for designers' innovative, even fantastical ideas, and the novel creations have captured the imagination and attention of both the press and the public. In 1950, an illuminated blanket of stars suspended above guests was arranged in the formation of the night sky at 9 p.m. on Christmas Eve. It was called the "Ceiling of Stars."

2006

1951

1954

As any holiday visitor knows, decorative celebrations of the season throughout Rockefeller Center are just as much a part of the experience there as the Tree. By the late 1950s, surrounding buildings began contributing to the wintry scene with their own decorations—many of which are now considered to be an essential part of the tradition. The façade of Saks Fifth Avenue provides a spectacular backdrop for the Tree. One year, the building was embellished with thirty-two-foot-high aluminum angels that were so dramatic they caused traffic jams along Fifth Avenue. These days, the building provides the canvas for a musical, dazzling animation of snowflakes.

Soldiers and Troubadours

Previous pages: Decorations span from Fifth Avenue to the Channel Gardens. *Left:* Karl Pehme's troubadours were made of fiberglass and sprayed with antique gold. Smaller figures of seated children and four colorful shields bearing yuletide and musical motifs mounted on poles completed the decorations along the Channel Gardens in 1965.

Some additions to the Rockefeller Center decor have
delighted onlookers for one brief festive season only;
others have endured and taken their place next to the
Tree, and in people's memories, as perennial holiday
institutions. From ambitious, spectacular creations
to the simple arrangements of crimson poinsettias
throughout the lobbies of the Center's buildings, these
extra elements embellish this epicenter of holiday
cheer. Over the years, they all have united to share one
special and comforting holiday message to visitors
from around the world: "The holidays have arrived."

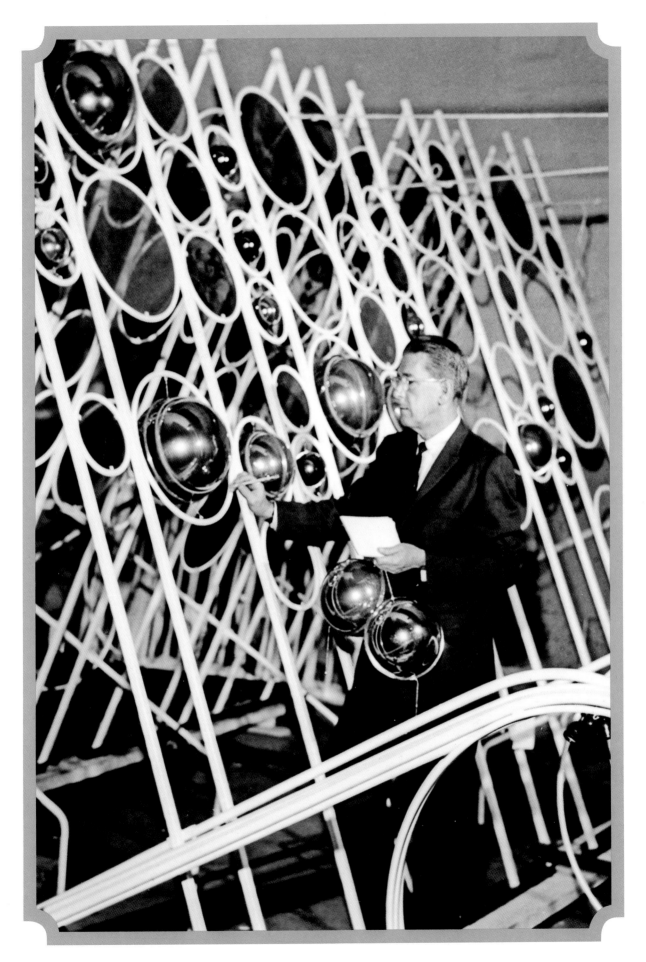

Valerie Clarebout

Sculptor Valerie Clarebout's triumphant and towering metal wire angel figures are such an intrinsic part of the Christmas experience at Rockefeller Center that many spectators find it hard to believe that anything else ever occupied the Channel Gardens and Promenade.

Decorations from both Clarebout and others filled these spaces over the years, and it was not until 1975 that the eight-foot-tall angels began their unbroken and perennial run as essential elements of the Center's holiday celebration.

A native of Surrey, England, Clarebout trained as a painter and sculptor at the Royal Academy of Art in London and Julien Studio in Paris. She moved to the United States in 1952. Clarebout's first contribution to the holiday scene was in 1954, when Robert Carson hired her to create a display of twelve nine-foot-tall angels crafted from hand-meshed aluminum wire and brass. She used eighteen miles of wire for the sculptures and 150 miniature lights to enhance the figures' robes. The angels came to the Channel Gardens in 1955, painted in colors inspired by the fifteenth-century Italian Renaissance artist della Robbia.

Clarebout created a new collection of decorations for the Center in 1958: a menagerie of fifty-four forest creatures made of brass and aluminum wire, inspired by the hymn "All Things Bright and Beautiful." The fanciful zoo included deer, fawns, rabbits, foxes, chipmunks, and even a skunk. The collection expanded in 1959, and the Plaza was filled with four eight-foot-tall wire trees and a staggering seventy-two animals adorned with 13,650 berry-bright red spangles.

Clarebout created several additional sculptures for the holiday season at Rockefeller Center, including snowmen sporting top hats, a dozen jack-in-the-box wire sculptures, and giant alphabet blocks. The current angels made their debut in 1969. The artist created the twelve sculptures in her New Fairfield, Connecticut, studio using seventy-five pounds of wire for each figure. (A total of seventy-six miles of wire was used in the creation of the display.) Delicately embroidered aluminum serves as the angels' hair, and each angel holds a six-foot-long brass trumpet. Wire snowflake sculptures ranging in height from three to eleven feet round out the collection.

It was a Christmas carol that provided the inspiration for the figures: "It came upon the midnight clear/That glorious song of old/From angels bending near the earth/To touch their harps of gold."

Valerie Clarebout died in 1982 at the age of seventy-four, but her legacy lives on in her resplendent gift to New York City. A year before her death, she was quoted in the *New York Times*, saying of the angels, "I love them. I love this time of year. Since I was a child I had a tremendous feeling for Christmas quite apart from a religious holiday. I used to lie on the ground and I thought I could feel the earth being reborn. That's how I always thought of Christmas—as the rebirth of the earth. And now, of course, every year I think of it as bringing the angels back to life."

THE CROWDS GATHER AT ROCKEFELLER CENTER
TO WITNESS THE TREE LIGHTING, 1961.

ROCKEFELLER Center's first publicity director, Merle Crowell, is credited with formalizing the tradition of a Christmas tree at Rockefeller Center. The first holiday program in 1933—the genesis of which was rooted firmly in the desire to generate press for the Center—consisted of a female trumpet trio, a performance by a local choir, and a national broadcast on NBC radio the following day.

Over the years, interest in the Tree and its lighting has increased exponentially, as have the crowds drawn to watch the Lighting Ceremony and the entertainment that goes along with the annual event. • The Tree Lighting reached more people than ever before in 1951, when the ceremony was first televised coast-to-coast on *The Kate Smith Evening Hour.* An estimated fourteen million viewers watched the Tree spring to illuminated life on *The Howdy Doody Show* in 1953.

Illuminating the Christmas Tree

Right, top: In 2005, the Lighting Ceremony featured the debut of the largest star to ever grace the Tree. *Bottom:* Crowds who gathered to watch the Tree Ceremony in 2001 witnessed a tribute to the heroes, traditions, strength, and unity of the United States after 9/11. First Lady Laura Bush was a special guest, and visitors filled the Plaza to hear (and to document) performances by Marc Anthony and Destiny's Child.

Hark! Hark!

In 1933, a stage was set on the Lower Plaza and the Paulist Choristers performed, beginning the tradition of musical performances to mark the lighting of the Tree.

ROCKEFELLER CENTER

FOR RELEASE
THURSDAY
-- DECEMBER 21, 1933.

The most elaborate program yet planned for the series of Christmastide festivities in the Sunken Plaza in Rockefeller Center will be held this afternoon (Thursday, December 21st) at 5 P.M. o'clock. It will feature the choir of The Church of The Heavenly Rest, one of the best trained male choirs in the country.

This program will be unusual in that the forty members of the choir, under the direction of James M. Helfenstein, will sing from the platform in the Sunken Plaza and be accompanied by Richard Liebert, organist, playing in the studio of the Radio City Music Hall. The organ music will be brought into the Sunken Plaza by wire and transmitted through the public address system used to amplify the singing. This accompaniment is made possible through a specially synchronized hook-up installed by the National Broadcasting Company which brings the singers in the Plaza into immediate connection with the organist.

The program this evening will be opened by the Gloria Trumpeters, as were the others in the series of carol singings that are being held each evening throughout the week in the Sunken Plaza. This will be followed by Mr. Liebert on the organ, and the choir.

The choir will march into the Sunken Plaza through a doorway from Rockefeller Concourse, the sub-surface level of the RCA Building, to the processional "Hark! Hark! My Soul." They will be preceded by an orthodox crucifer bearing the crucifix and a standard-

Awestruck

A gift from the state of Vermont, the 1957 Tree was festooned with 1,100 custom-designed twelve- and eighteen-inch lanterns in multiple colors, and three thousand 7-watt firefly lights.

Hosts of the Lighting Ceremony include some of the most popular and legendary entertainment personalities of their time. Ann Curry, Al Roker, Johnny Carson, Phil Donahue, Tony Bennett, Merv Griffin, and Liza Minnelli have all presided over the holiday tradition. In 1991, Lucie Arnaz sang her rendition of "White Christmas" in a torrential rain; host Glenn Close sang "Away in a Manger" at the conclusion of the 1992 ceremony; and Christopher Reeve read "'Twas the Night Before Christmas" at the 1994 event.

Voices Raised in Song

Yet another brainchild of the Center's director of
publicity, Merle Crowell, was the Rockefeller Center
Choristers. The choral group, founded in 1939, at
times numbered two hundred strong and was made
up of Center employees from all walks of life.

CANDLELIGHT CONCERTS of
Christmas Carols
ROCKEFELLER CENTER CHORISTERS

On the Skating Pond
THURS. DEC. 23 6 to 6:30 PM.
"CHRISTMAS ICE CARNIVAL"
with stars from
"HOWDY MR. ICE"

LOWER PLAZA
WEDNESDAY
DEC. 22
at
5:30 to 6 PM

THURSDAY
DEC. 23

In 1958, adagio skaters Nancy Lee Parker and Nicky Powers took to the ice.

Every year hundreds of amateur skaters try to keep their balance on blades as Prometheus looks on.

CHRISTMAS AT ROCKEFELLER CENTER, '64
PRODUCER-DIRECTOR: DAN PETERS
WRITER: GENE FELDMAN
ASSOCIATE PRODUCER: RAYSA BONOW
                    AIR 12/10/64-6:15-6:30 p.m.

VIDEO	AUDIO

PENSACOLA CHOIR

WIDE SHOT ON
CHANNEL GARDENS

SUPER TITLES
LOSE TITLES

JACK IN THE BOXES

CHOIR: OPENING CAROL

JOHNNY CARSON: (VO)

Christmas in New York —1964

(LOSE CHOIR)

MS CARSON

JOHNNY CARSON

Hello, I'm Johnny Carson, greeting you tonight
from a widdy vantage point in the Lower Plaza
here in Rockefeller Center where shortly we wi
see the lighting of the giant Christmas tree—
an unchanging event which takes places every
year in the very heart of a city noted more fo
its change than its custom.

What with New York City changing its face so
often it's sometimes hard to recognize "The Bi
Town" from day to day—buildings being torn
down, new ones going up—it's kind of good to
have some things that aren't changing. It's

110

Giving the Tree life through the pressing of the Button (although in 2001 the switch was a giant candy cane) is, of course, a coveted role. Over the years, many of the families who donated their trees have had the honor of assisting. In 1971, perhaps as a sort of consolation prize, fifteen Cub Scouts participated in the Lighting after their effort to find a Rockefeller Center–worthy tree in their Brooklyn neighborhood of Bedford-Stuyvesant was unsuccessful. Among the V.I.P.s invited to light the Tree in recent years were First Lady Hillary Clinton, First Lady Laura Bush, and Bernie Williams and Paul O'Neill, members of the 1999 World Champion New York Yankees.

Here's Johnny!

Below: Johnny Carson was master of ceremonies in 1964 and presided over the Lighting with his usual sense of humor. *Left:* His television script for the evening's ceremony.

HOWDY DOODY

CLARABELL
THE CLOWN

NATALIE COLE

JEAN MADEIRA AND
COLLIN DRIGGS

SARAH
MACLACHLAN

NICK LACHEY

TAYLOR HICKS

ALTON G. MARSHALL
AND BARBARA
WALTERS

LIONEL RICHIE

PAUL TRIPP

PAUL LAVALLE

LILY TOMLIN

MICKEY MOUSE

TONY BENNETT

DONALD DUCK

Right, clockwise from top left: *Arthur Godfrey, 98 Degrees, Collin Driggs and Jean Madeira, and Destiny's Child.*

ROCKEFEL

KOREAN
ORCHESTRA
6 piece

CHOR

LITTLE
ANGELS PROME
DANCERS

International Influences

Background: The floor plan for the 1971 ceremony includes mention of
the Button, as well as the schedule for the skating segment of the
evening. *Right:* Little Angels of Korea, members of the National Folk
Ballet of Korea, performed a traditional drum dance as part of the
evening's entertainment.

SKATING

① SKAT

② SNO

③ SANT

④ F

ORGAN

2 STEP
RISER

5R0UB

BUTTON
AREA

HOST
LECTURN

FOUNTAIN WILLIAM
WALKER

PLAZA

Top left: The Police Athletic League Steel Band, an East Harlem youth group, performed a calypso medley of holiday favorites in front of the Tree in 1971. *Bottom left:* Also in 1971, the Uniroyal Glee Club and the Wasa Swedish Folk Group presented the Swedish custom of Lucia Day along the Promenade. The role of Lucia was played by the Swedish model Christina Lang.

Throughout the years, a crucial part of the pageantry at Rockefeller Center—both at the Lighting Ceremony and throughout the season—is the wide array of entertainment. • Music has always played a central role in the holiday celebrations. Early traditions included performances by glee clubs and children's choirs. Another tribute in song is the annual TubaChristmas concert, a brassy convocation conceived in 1974 that has drawn as many as five hundred tubas and euphoniums to perform Christmas carols on the Rink. Some of the country's most popular and celebrated entertainers have performed at the base of the majestic Tree over the years, including Sting, John Mayer, Mariah Carey, Mel Tormé, 'N Sync, Sheryl Crow, and Destiny's Child.

TubaChristmas

Another long-running holiday tradition at Rockefeller Center
is the annual TubaChristmas, founded in 1974.

Pushing the Magic Button

Right: Sisters Eileen and Peggy Murphy pressed the Button to light the Tree in 1949; their father, John Murphy, worked in the Protection Department at Rockefeller Center. *Far right*: Posing in front of the 1969 Tree are Saranac Lake, New York, Mayor Alton B. Anderson; two of the town's peewee Hockey players who discovered the Tree; Rockefeller Center president G. S. Eyssell; and Joseph Reilly, chairman of the Saranac Lake tree selection committee. *Bottom right*: In 1964 singers Ed Powell and Mira Hinson performed as Mr. and Mrs. Santa Claus.

Once a fifteen-minute interruption of local New York City programming, the Lighting of the Christmas Tree at Rockefeller Center is now a much-anticipated, two-hour, star-studded, live television event that reaches millions. If history is any guide, these numbers, and the affection for the Tree, will only continue to grow in the years to come.

CROWDS GATHER IN FRONT OF THE UNLIT TREE, 1938.

IT is said that no matter how many times you've seen a photograph of the Christmas Tree at Rockefeller Center, nothing compares to seeing it in person. The Tree's imposing and singular form, the dazzling spectrum of lights, and Valerie Clarebout's resplendent angels are nothing short of breathtaking when the great evergreen gleams above in the night. With the hustle and bustle of busy holiday shoppers completing the picture, the Plaza is an epicenter of holiday cheer.

Old Saint Nick

Right, top: In 1936, a Santa's Workshop was set up in the International Building where employees wrapped three thousand gifts. Rockefeller employees Bill Steinke and Elizabeth Harden played Mr. and Mrs. Claus. On Christmas Eve, they handed out gifts to five hundred underprivileged children at a party held in the Lower Plaza. *Bottom*: Broadway, film, and television actor Joseph Hardy played Santa Claus in 1972, strolling throughout the Center and giving out gifts and candy to children.

Millions of people come from around the world to gaze upon the spectacular sight, participate in the Tree Lighting, take photos of loved ones, or just enjoy a brief pause in the hectic schedule of the holiday season. A quarter of New York City's tourists visit between the beginning of November and New Year's, and the shining Tree is one of the city's biggest draws.

A few pilgrimages to the Tree have even secured a place in its history. Rockefeller Center's Skating Rink debuted in 1936. Omero C. Catan, widely known as "Mr. First" due to his determination to be the first person to attend any event or opening in New York, set his sights on Rockefeller Center. When the Rink opened, Catan was the first to take to the ice.

A World of Visitors

People from all walks of life come to visit the Tree at Rockefeller Center, from school groups to foreign Naval legions.

In 1940, less than a decade into the tenure of the Tree
at Rockefeller Center, the *New York Times* was already
referring to the evergreen as "a New York institution,"
describing it as a destination for "homesick visitors"
or New Yorkers "in search of a lift for war-weary
spirits." In 1945, a G.I. who had been stationed in the
South Pacific for four years stood beneath the Tree.
"A real Christmas," he remarked. "No palm trees."

The Skating Rink

Opened in 1936, the Ice Skating Rink at Rockefeller Center provides
a unique vantage point from which to view the Tree. *Following pages:*
Skaters glide beneath the 1981 Tree. A pair of Trees presided over the
Rink in its first year.

Holiday Reverie

A young couple takes a quiet moment among
the crowds of the Promenade in 1971.

Over the years, thousands of international media
outlets have been on hand to report the story of the
season. • Special guests with a little more invested
in the display are the families who donate their tree
and take in the majestic sight with tremendous pride.
• The Christmas Tree at Rockefeller Center has the
ability to enchant both lifetime enthusiasts and first-
time visitors. Often, one visit to the Tree plants the
seeds for many more, making a holiday appearance
at Rockefeller Center a steadfast tradition for tourists
and New Yorkers alike.

1968 *This year's theme was a holiday festival inspired by the eighteenth century, including sculptures of a town crier, merry musicians, and frolicking children.*

Childhood Memories

The Christmas Tree at Rockefeller Center holds a special place in the hearts of children who see its breathtaking grandeur firsthand.

The Legacy

Yesterday and Today

Right: Tree from 1933. *Following page:* Tree from 2006

Over the past decades, the Christmas Tree at Rockefeller Center has taken many forms: a virtually improvised gesture of holiday spirit in the depths of the Depression, a symbol of unity and cheer during wartime, and, of course, its most enduring incarnation as an icon of the holiday season that's both beloved and recognized around the world. The most famous Christmas Tree in the world will surely continue to gain more fans with each passing year, with its legacy shining ever brighter because of them.

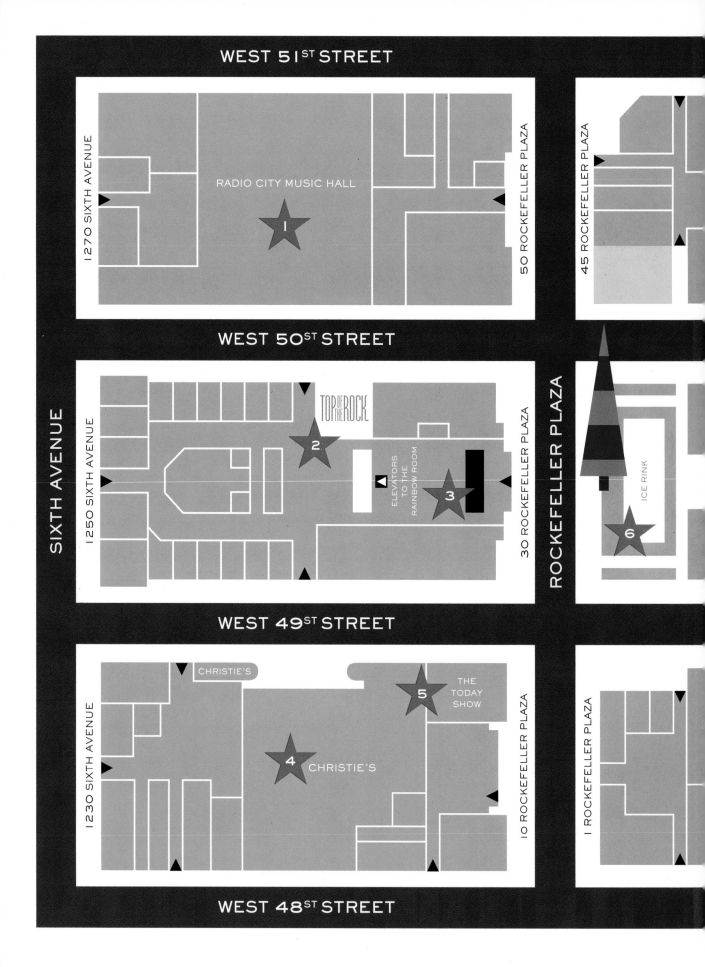

WEST 51ST STREET

1270 SIXTH AVENUE

RADIO CITY MUSIC HALL

1

50 ROCKEFELLER PLAZA

45 ROCKEFELLER PLAZA

WEST 50ST STREET

SIXTH AVENUE

1250 SIXTH AVENUE

TOP OF THE ROCK

2

ELEVATORS TO THE RAINBOW ROOM

3

30 ROCKEFELLER PLAZA

ROCKEFELLER PLAZA

ICE RINK

6

WEST 49ST STREET

1230 SIXTH AVENUE

CHRISTIE'S

4 CHRISTIE'S

5 THE TODAY SHOW

10 ROCKEFELLER PLAZA

1 ROCKEFELLER PLAZA

WEST 48ST STREET

142

WEST 51ST STREET

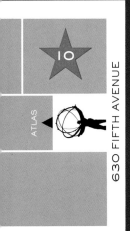

10

ATLAS

630 FIFTH AVENUE

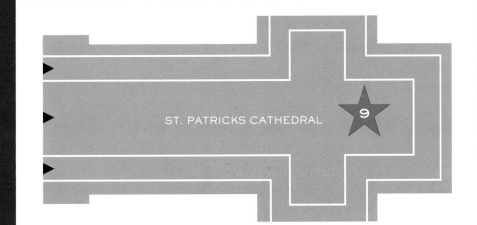

ST. PATRICKS CATHEDRAL

9

WEST 50ST STREET

620 FIFTH AVENUE

CHANNEL GARDENS

7

610 FIFTH AVENUE

FIFTH AVENUE

611 FIFTH AVENUE

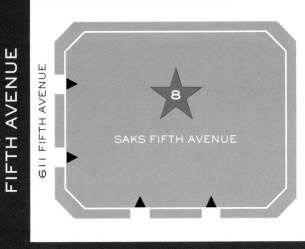

8

SAKS FIFTH AVENUE

WEST 49ST STREET

600 FIFTH AVENUE

Map of Rockefeller Center

★ 1. Radio City Music Hall
★ 2. Top of the Rock
★ 3. The Rainbow Room
★ 4. Christies
★ 5. The Today Show
★ 6. The Rink
★ 7. The Channel Gardens
★ 8. Saks Fifth Avenue
★ 9. St. Patrick's Cathedral
★ 10. Atlas

TISHMAN SPEYER WOULD LIKE TO THANK BART BARLOW, DAN OKRENT, CHRISTINE ROUSSEL,
AND THE ROCKEFELLER CENTER ARCHIVES.

MELCHER MEDIA WOULD LIKE TO THANK TISHMAN SPEYER, RUBENSTEIN ASSOCIATES,
WILLIAM BOSTWICK, DAVID E. BROWN, DANIEL DEL VALLE, MAX J. DICKSTEIN, LAUREN NATHAN,
LIA RONNEN, HOLLY ROTHMAN, JESSI RYMILL, ALEX TART, SHOSHANA THALER, MARTI TRGOVICH,
SAMANTHA WOLF, BETTY WONG, AND MEGAN WORMAN.

PHOTOS COURTESY OF TISHMAN SPEYER, PHOTOGRAPHER BART BARLOW: 20-21 (1997-2006),
24 (bottom right), 36-37, 38-39, 42 (bottom), 43 (bottom), 60-61, 64, 65, 67, 70-71, 74-75, 79, 86, 90, 101,
112 (second row, right; third row, middle and right; fourth row, left and second from right), 113 (top right,
bottom left), 118 (bottom), 119, 130-131, 140-141

PHOTOS © ROCKEFELLER GROUP, INC: 2, 8, 11, 12, 13, 14-15, 16-17, 18-19 (1972-1984, 1987), 20-21 (1991,
1993, 1994) 22, 24 (top, bottom right), 26, 27, 29, 30, 32, 33, 34, 40-41, 44, 50, 52, 53, 57, 59, 62, 68, 73, 76,
77, 78, 83, 84, 85, 87, 89, 91, 92, 95, 96, 98, 102, 104, 106-107, 108-109, 111, 112 (second row, left; third row,
left; fourth row, second from left and last; fifth row, left, middle, right), 113 (top left, bottom right), 115, 116,
120-121, 122, 125, 126, 129, 132, 133, 135, 139

DOCUMENTS APPEARING ON THE FOLLOWING PAGES ARE COURTESY OF THE ROCKEFELLER CENTER
ARCHIVES: 7, 69, 103, 107, 110, 112 (top), 114-115

PHOTOS © BART BARLOW: 18-19 (1985, 1986, 1988, 1989), 20-21 (1990, 1992), 25, 54-55, 72, 80, 82, 112
(fifth row, second from left and second from right), 118 (top), 136, 137

PHOTOS © AP/WIDEWORLD: 20 (1996): MARK LENNIHAN; 21 (1995): ADAM NADEL;
42-43: WALLY SANTANA; 43: MITSU YASUKAWA